Project Management Checklist
Step By Step Project Management Activities

List of activities under Initiation, Planning, Execution, Monitoring & Control, Closing

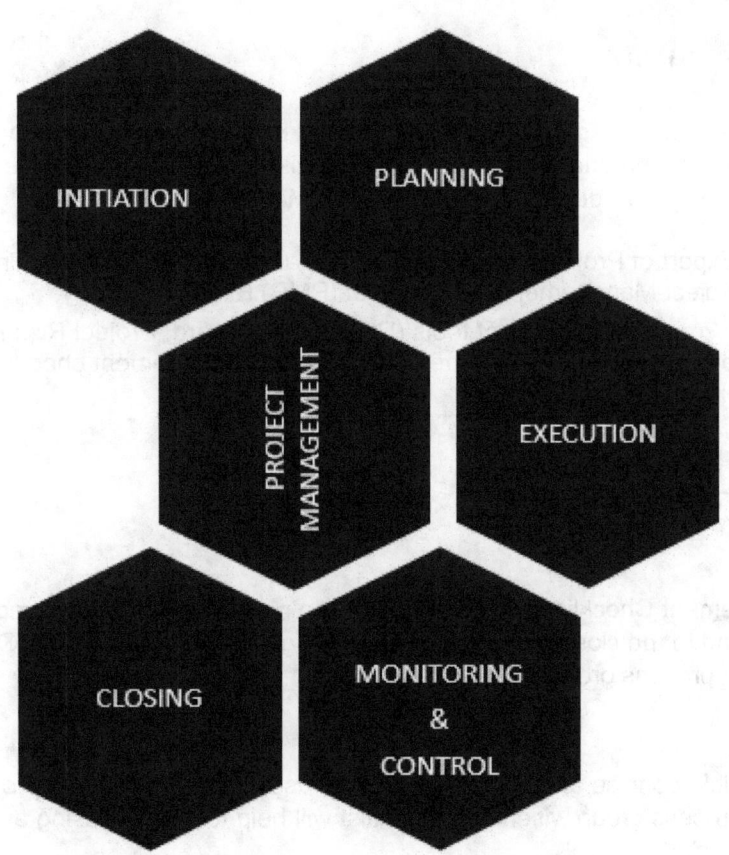

N.U.Rehman, MS, PMP

About the Author

Over 20 years of professional consulting and academic experience across Canada, Middle East (UAE) & other countries. Results Oriented Professional with exceptional Management System, Project Management, Consulting, Training and Auditing experience.

Graduation in Civil Engineering and completed MS degree with specialization in Project Management from the University of Alberta, Canada.

▶ Professional designations:

- Project Management Professional (PMP) ®
- ISO 9001, 14001, 18001- Certified Lead Auditor

More about the author

Rehman is Senior Project Manager and former Assistant Professor at Engineering University and delivered lectures to undergraduate students and supervised their undergraduate final year projects. He also provided trainings to Adult Learners on Project Management.

- Subject Matter Expert of Project Management (Fundamental & Advanced), Project Risk Management, Project Management Professional (PMP) Exam.
- Created PMO & Project management tools (Project Dashboard, Project Risk register, Stakeholder analysis tool, Communication management tool, Project management checklist, RACI Matrix, Project Post-mortem, Project Charter)

About Handbook:

This Project Management Checklist provide step by step project activities required to execute the project from beginning to the closeout. This handbook aligns with PMI's PMBOK® and covers all project management process group.

This checklist is flexible concise and comprehensive to use in different type of projects. All project activities list down process group wise. This checklist will help to avoid missing any activity during the execution of the project.

Project Title	
Project No:	
Client Information	
Client Project Manager	
Company Project Manager	
Project Start Date	
Project End Date	

PROJECT MANAGEMENT CHECKLIST-STEP BY STEP PROJECT ACTIVITIES

No.	Project Stage	Process Group	Checklist	Status Yes/No/NA	Targeted Time	Date
1		Initiation	Contract Review			
2		Initiation	Open Project in system			
3		Initiation	Request for creating Project Home (folder) and request to assign Project Administrator			
4		Initiation	Request for Performance Bond to Finance (if applicable)			
5		Initiation	Request for Advance Payment Bond to Finance (if applicable)			
6		Initiation	Prepare Project Charter			
7		Initiation	Identify Stakeholders and prepare Stakeholder management plan			
8		Initiation	Obtain Project Resources (Team)-Mobilisation			
9		Initiation	External Kick off Meeting with Client			
10		Initiation	Internal Kick off Meeting with Project Team and Management			
11		Initiation	Scope Verification			
12		Initiation	Set Project KPIs			

PROJECT MANAGEMENT CHECKLIST-STEP BY STEP PROJECT ACTIVITIES

No.	Project Stage	Process Group	Checklist	Status Yes/No/NA	Targeted Time	Date
13		Initiation	Data Collection			
14		Initiation	Issue Notice of Intent			
15		Planning	Prepare RACI Matrix			
16		Planning	Set Project Communication Protocol & Prepare Communication Management Plan			
17		Planning	Prepare Project Management Plan			
18		Planning	Approval of Project Plan (Internal/external)			
19		Planning	Prepare Baseline Schedule			
20		Planning	Prepare Project Budget			
21		Planning	Prepare List of Deliverables			
22		Planning	Prepare Document Control Register			
23		Planning	Identify Initial Project Risks			
24		Planning	Prepare Risk Register			

PROJECT MANAGEMENT CHECKLIST-STEP BY STEP PROJECT ACTIVITIES

No.	Project Stage	Process Group	Checklist	Status Yes/No/NA	Targeted Time	Date
25		Planning	Prepare Inter Discipline document squad check			
26		Planning	Prepare Document Control List			
27		Planning	Prepare Project Documents Checker and approver List			
28		Execution	Monthly Progress Report (External)			
29		Execution	Weekly/Bi weekly Progress Report			
30		Execution	Internal Progress Meeting			
31		Execution	External Progress Meeting			
32		Execution	MOMs (Internal & External meetings)			
33		Execution	Prepare stage wise Design Reports			
34		Execution	Prepare BOQ & Tender Documents			
35		Execution	Prepare Cost Estimate			
36		Monitoring & Control	Project Design Gate Reviews (at each stage)			

PROJECT MANAGEMENT CHECKLIST-STEP BY STEP PROJECT ACTIVITIES

No.	Project Stage	Process Group	Checklist	Status Yes/No/NA	Targeted Time	Date
37		Monitoring & Control	Review Risk list and update Risk Register (Each Stage of the Project)			
38		Execution	Lesson Learned Sessions (Each Stage of Project)			
39		Monitoring & Control	Project Internal Audit after 50% project completion			
40		Monitoring & Control	Update Project Financial Forecast			
41		Monitoring & Control	Prepare Justification or prepare recovery plan If project slips or creep			
42		Monitoring & Control	Monitor Man-Hours & Budget spent			
43		Monitoring & Control	Monitor Project Progress			
44		Monitoring & Control	Evaluate Scope change (if any)			
45		Monitoring & Control	Get approval of scope change from client			
46		Monitoring & Control	Implement only approved changes			
47		Close out	Send CSR (Client Satisfaction Report) to client			
48		Close out	Evaluate CSR with Management			

PROJECT MANAGEMENT CHECKLIST-STEP BY STEP PROJECT ACTIVITIES

No.	Project Stage	Process Group	Checklist	Status Yes/No/NA	Targeted Time	Date
49		Close out	Prepare Close out Report			
50		Close out	Project Post Mortem			
51		Close out	Ensure all invoices have been paid			
52		Close out	Complete job completion form			
53		Close out	Request the project closure			
54		Close out	Project Archiving			
55		Finance	Generate Invoices			
56		Finance	Follow-up with Finance and Client			
57	❖ Milestone	Execution	Submission of Design Reports to Client			
58	❖ Milestone	Execution	Submission of BOQ & Cost Estimate to Client			
59	❖ Mile Stone	Execution	Submission of Tender Documents to Client			
60	❖ Mile Stone	Execution	Documents submission to Authorities for obtaining NOCs			
61	❖ Mile Stone	Execution	Obtain Approvals from Authorities			
62	❖ Mile Stone	Execution	Obtain Approvals from Client			

PROJECT MANAGEMENT CHECKLIST-STEP BY STEP PROJECT ACTIVITIES

No.	Project Stage	Process Group	Checklist	Status Yes/No/NA	Targeted Time	Date
63						
64						
65						
66						
67						
68						
69						
70						
71						
72						
73						
74						
75						
76						

❖ Blank sheet provide for extra activities

Project Title	
Project No:	
Client Information	
Client Project Manager	
Company Project Manager	
Project Start Date	
Project End Date	

PROJECT MANAGEMENT CHECKLIST-STEP BY STEP PROJECT ACTIVITIES

No.	Project Stage	Process Group	Checklist	Status Yes/No/NA	Targeted Time	Date
1		Initiation	Contract Review			
2		Initiation	Open Project in system			
3		Initiation	Request for creating Project Home (folder) and request to assign Project Administrator			
4		Initiation	Request for Performance Bond to Finance (if applicable)			
5		Initiation	Request for Advance Payment Bond to Finance (if applicable)			
6		Initiation	Prepare Project Charter			
7		Initiation	Identify Stakeholders and prepare Stakeholder management plan			
8		Initiation	Obtain Project Resources (Team)-Mobilisation			
9		Initiation	External Kick off Meeting with Client			
10		Initiation	Internal Kick off Meeting with Project Team and Management			
11		Initiation	Scope Verification			
12		Initiation	Set Project KPIs			

PROJECT MANAGEMENT CHECKLIST-STEP BY STEP PROJECT ACTIVITIES

No.	Project Stage	Process Group	Checklist	Status Yes/No/NA	Targeted Time	Date
13		Initiation	Data Collection			
14		Initiation	Issue Notice of Intent			
15		Planning	Prepare RACI Matrix			
16		Planning	Set Project Communication Protocol & Prepare Communication Management Plan			
17		Planning	Prepare Project Management Plan			
18		Planning	Approval of Project Plan (Internal/external)			
19		Planning	Prepare Baseline Schedule			
20		Planning	Prepare Project Budget			
21		Planning	Prepare List of Deliverables			
22		Planning	Prepare Document Control Register			
23		Planning	Identify Initial Project Risks			
24		Planning	Prepare Risk Register			

PROJECT MANAGEMENT CHECKLIST-STEP BY STEP PROJECT ACTIVITIES

No.	Project Stage	Process Group	Checklist	Status Yes/No/NA	Targeted Time	Date
25		Planning	Prepare Inter Discipline document squad check			
26		Planning	Prepare Document Control List			
27		Planning	Prepare Project Documents Checker and approver List			
28		Execution	Monthly Progress Report (External)			
29		Execution	Weekly/Bi weekly Progress Report			
30		Execution	Internal Progress Meeting			
31		Execution	External Progress Meeting			
32		Execution	MOMs (Internal & External meetings)			
33		Execution	Prepare stage wise Design Reports			
34		Execution	Prepare BOQ & Tender Documents			
35		Execution	Prepare Cost Estimate			
36		Monitoring & Control	Project Design Gate Reviews (at each stage)			

PROJECT MANAGEMENT CHECKLIST-STEP BY STEP PROJECT ACTIVITIES

No.	Project Stage	Process Group	Checklist	Status Yes/No/NA	Targeted Time	Date
37		Monitoring & Control	Review Risk list and update Risk Register (Each Stage of the Project)			
38		Execution	Lesson Learned Sessions (Each Stage of Project)			
39		Monitoring & Control	Project Internal Audit after 50% project completion			
40		Monitoring & Control	Update Project Financial Forecast			
41		Monitoring & Control	Prepare Justification or prepare recovery plan If project slips or creep			
42		Monitoring & Control	Monitor Man-Hours & Budget spent			
43		Monitoring & Control	Monitor Project Progress			
44		Monitoring & Control	Evaluate Scope change (if any)			
45		Monitoring & Control	Get approval of scope change from client			
46		Monitoring & Control	Implement only approved changes			
47		Close out	Send CSR (Client Satisfaction Report) to client			
48		Close out	Evaluate CSR with Management			

PROJECT MANAGEMENT CHECKLIST-STEP BY STEP PROJECT ACTIVITIES

No.	Project Stage	Process Group	Checklist	Status Yes/No/NA	Targeted Time	Date
49		Close out	Prepare Close out Report			
50		Close out	Project Post Mortem			
51		Close out	Ensure all invoices have been paid			
52		Close out	Complete job completion form			
53		Close out	Request the project closure			
54		Close out	Project Archiving			
55		Finance	Generate Invoices			
56		Finance	Follow-up with Finance and Client			
57	❖ Milestone	Execution	Submission of Design Reports to Client			
58	❖ Milestone	Execution	Submission of BOQ & Cost Estimate to Client			
59	❖ Mile Stone	Execution	Submission of Tender Documents to Client			
60	❖ Mile Stone	Execution	Documents submission to Authorities for obtaining NOCs			
61	❖ Mile Stone	Execution	Obtain Approvals from Authorities			
62	❖ Mile Stone	Execution	Obtain Approvals from Client			

PROJECT MANAGEMENT CHECKLIST-STEP BY STEP PROJECT ACTIVITIES

No.	Project Stage	Process Group	Checklist	Status Yes/No/NA	Targeted Time	Date
63						
64						
65						
66						
67						
68						
69						
70						
71						
72						
73						
74						
75						
76						

❖ Blank sheet provide for extra activities

Project Title	
Project No:	
Client Information	
Client Project Manager	
Company Project Manager	
Project Start Date	
Project End Date	

PROJECT MANAGEMENT CHECKLIST-STEP BY STEP PROJECT ACTIVITIES

No.	Project Stage	Process Group	Checklist	Status Yes/No/NA	Targeted Time	Date
1		Initiation	Contract Review			
2		Initiation	Open Project in system			
3		Initiation	Request for creating Project Home (folder) and request to assign Project Administrator			
4		Initiation	Request for Performance Bond to Finance (if applicable)			
5		Initiation	Request for Advance Payment Bond to Finance (if applicable)			
6		Initiation	Prepare Project Charter			
7		Initiation	Identify Stakeholders and prepare Stakeholder management plan			
8		Initiation	Obtain Project Resources (Team)-Mobilisation			
9		Initiation	External Kick off Meeting with Client			
10		Initiation	Internal Kick off Meeting with Project Team and Management			
11		Initiation	Scope Verification			
12		Initiation	Set Project KPIs			

PROJECT MANAGEMENT CHECKLIST-STEP BY STEP PROJECT ACTIVITIES

No.	Project Stage	Process Group	Checklist	Status Yes/No/NA	Targeted Time	Date
13		Initiation	Data Collection			
14		Initiation	Issue Notice of Intent			
15		Planning	Prepare RACI Matrix			
16		Planning	Set Project Communication Protocol & Prepare Communication Management Plan			
17		Planning	Prepare Project Management Plan			
18		Planning	Approval of Project Plan (Internal/external)			
19		Planning	Prepare Baseline Schedule			
20		Planning	Prepare Project Budget			
21		Planning	Prepare List of Deliverables			
22		Planning	Prepare Document Control Register			
23		Planning	Identify Initial Project Risks			
24		Planning	Prepare Risk Register			

PROJECT MANAGEMENT CHECKLIST-STEP BY STEP PROJECT ACTIVITIES

No.	Project Stage	Process Group	Checklist	Status Yes/No/NA	Targeted Time	Date
25		Planning	Prepare Inter Discipline document squad check			
26		Planning	Prepare Document Control List			
27		Planning	Prepare Project Documents Checker and approver List			
28		Execution	Monthly Progress Report (External)			
29		Execution	Weekly/Bi weekly Progress Report			
30		Execution	Internal Progress Meeting			
31		Execution	External Progress Meeting			
32		Execution	MOMs (Internal & External meetings)			
33		Execution	Prepare stage wise Design Reports			
34		Execution	Prepare BOQ & Tender Documents			
35		Execution	Prepare Cost Estimate			
36		Monitoring & Control	Project Design Gate Reviews (at each stage)			

PROJECT MANAGEMENT CHECKLIST-STEP BY STEP PROJECT ACTIVITIES

No.	Project Stage	Process Group	Checklist	Status Yes/No/NA	Targeted Time	Date
37		Monitoring & Control	Review Risk list and update Risk Register (Each Stage of the Project)			
38		Execution	Lesson Learned Sessions (Each Stage of Project)			
39		Monitoring & Control	Project Internal Audit after 50% project completion			
40		Monitoring & Control	Update Project Financial Forecast			
41		Monitoring & Control	Prepare Justification or prepare recovery plan If project slips or creep			
42		Monitoring & Control	Monitor Man-Hours & Budget spent			
43		Monitoring & Control	Monitor Project Progress			
44		Monitoring & Control	Evaluate Scope change (if any)			
45		Monitoring & Control	Get approval of scope change from client			
46		Monitoring & Control	Implement only approved changes			
47		Close out	Send CSR (Client Satisfaction Report) to client			
48		Close out	Evaluate CSR with Management			

PROJECT MANAGEMENT CHECKLIST-STEP BY STEP PROJECT ACTIVITIES

No.	Project Stage	Process Group	Checklist	Status Yes/No/NA	Targeted Time	Date
49		Close out	Prepare Close out Report			
50		Close out	Project Post Mortem			
51		Close out	Ensure all invoices have been paid			
52		Close out	Complete job completion form			
53		Close out	Request the project closure			
54		Close out	Project Archiving			
55		Finance	Generate Invoices			
56		Finance	Follow-up with Finance and Client			
57	❖ Milestone	Execution	Submission of Design Reports to Client			
58	❖ Milestone	Execution	Submission of BOQ & Cost Estimate to Client			
59	❖ Mile Stone	Execution	Submission of Tender Documents to Client			
60	❖ Mile Stone	Execution	Documents submission to Authorities for obtaining NOCs			
61	❖ Mile Stone	Execution	Obtain Approvals from Authorities			
62	❖ Mile Stone	Execution	Obtain Approvals from Client			

PROJECT MANAGEMENT CHECKLIST-STEP BY STEP PROJECT ACTIVITIES

No.	Project Stage	Process Group	Checklist	Status Yes/No/NA	Targeted Time	Date
63						
64						
65						
66						
67						
68						
69						
70						
71						
72						
73						
74						
75						
76						

❖ Blank sheet provide for extra activities

Project Title	
Project No:	
Client Information	
Client Project Manager	
Company Project Manager	
Project Start Date	
Project End Date	

PROJECT MANAGEMENT CHECKLIST-STEP BY STEP PROJECT ACTIVITIES

No.	Project Stage	Process Group	Checklist	Status Yes/No/NA	Targeted Time	Date
1		Initiation	Contract Review			
2		Initiation	Open Project in system			
3		Initiation	Request for creating Project Home (folder) and request to assign Project Administrator			
4		Initiation	Request for Performance Bond to Finance (if applicable)			
5		Initiation	Request for Advance Payment Bond to Finance (if applicable)			
6		Initiation	Prepare Project Charter			
7		Initiation	Identify Stakeholders and prepare Stakeholder management plan			
8		Initiation	Obtain Project Resources (Team)-Mobilisation			
9		Initiation	External Kick off Meeting with Client			
10		Initiation	Internal Kick off Meeting with Project Team and Management			
11		Initiation	Scope Verification			
12		Initiation	Set Project KPIs			

PROJECT MANAGEMENT CHECKLIST-STEP BY STEP PROJECT ACTIVITIES

No.	Project Stage	Process Group	Checklist	Status Yes/No/NA	Targeted Time	Date
13		Initiation	Data Collection			
14		Initiation	Issue Notice of Intent			
15		Planning	Prepare RACI Matrix			
16		Planning	Set Project Communication Protocol & Prepare Communication Management Plan			
17		Planning	Prepare Project Management Plan			
18		Planning	Approval of Project Plan (Internal/external)			
19		Planning	Prepare Baseline Schedule			
20		Planning	Prepare Project Budget			
21		Planning	Prepare List of Deliverables			
22		Planning	Prepare Document Control Register			
23		Planning	Identify Initial Project Risks			
24		Planning	Prepare Risk Register			

PROJECT MANAGEMENT CHECKLIST-STEP BY STEP PROJECT ACTIVITIES

No.	Project Stage	Process Group	Checklist	Status Yes/No/NA	Targeted Time	Date
25		Planning	Prepare Inter Discipline document squad check			
26		Planning	Prepare Document Control List			
27		Planning	Prepare Project Documents Checker and approver List			
28		Execution	Monthly Progress Report (External)			
29		Execution	Weekly/Bi weekly Progress Report			
30		Execution	Internal Progress Meeting			
31		Execution	External Progress Meeting			
32		Execution	MOMs (Internal & External meetings)			
33		Execution	Prepare stage wise Design Reports			
34		Execution	Prepare BOQ & Tender Documents			
35		Execution	Prepare Cost Estimate			
36		Monitoring & Control	Project Design Gate Reviews (at each stage)			

PROJECT MANAGEMENT CHECKLIST-STEP BY STEP PROJECT ACTIVITIES

No.	Project Stage	Process Group	Checklist	Status Yes/No/NA	Targeted Time	Date
37		Monitoring & Control	Review Risk list and update Risk Register (Each Stage of the Project)			
38		Execution	Lesson Learned Sessions (Each Stage of Project)			
39		Monitoring & Control	Project Internal Audit after 50% project completion			
40		Monitoring & Control	Update Project Financial Forecast			
41		Monitoring & Control	Prepare Justification or prepare recovery plan If project slips or creep			
42		Monitoring & Control	Monitor Man-Hours & Budget spent			
43		Monitoring & Control	Monitor Project Progress			
44		Monitoring & Control	Evaluate Scope change (if any)			
45		Monitoring & Control	Get approval of scope change from client			
46		Monitoring & Control	Implement only approved changes			
47		Close out	Send CSR (Client Satisfaction Report) to client			
48		Close out	Evaluate CSR with Management			

PROJECT MANAGEMENT CHECKLIST-STEP BY STEP PROJECT ACTIVITIES

No.	Project Stage	Process Group	Checklist	Status Yes/No/NA	Targeted Time	Date
49		Close out	Prepare Close out Report			
50		Close out	Project Post Mortem			
51		Close out	Ensure all invoices have been paid			
52		Close out	Complete job completion form			
53		Close out	Request the project closure			
54		Close out	Project Archiving			
55		Finance	Generate Invoices			
56		Finance	Follow-up with Finance and Client			
57	❖ Milestone	Execution	Submission of Design Reports to Client			
58	❖ Milestone	Execution	Submission of BOQ & Cost Estimate to Client			
59	❖ Mile Stone	Execution	Submission of Tender Documents to Client			
60	❖ Mile Stone	Execution	Documents submission to Authorities for obtaining NOCs			
61	❖ Mile Stone	Execution	Obtain Approvals from Authorities			
62	❖ Mile Stone	Execution	Obtain Approvals from Client			

PROJECT MANAGEMENT CHECKLIST-STEP BY STEP PROJECT ACTIVITIES

No.	Project Stage	Process Group	Checklist	Status Yes/No/NA	Targeted Time	Date
63						
64						
65						
66						
67						
68						
69						
70						
71						
72						
73						
74						
75						
76						

❖ Blank sheet provide for extra activities

Project Title	
Project No:	
Client Information	
Client Project Manager	
Company Project Manager	
Project Start Date	
Project End Date	

PROJECT MANAGEMENT CHECKLIST-STEP BY STEP PROJECT ACTIVITIES

No.	Project Stage	Process Group	Checklist	Status Yes/No/NA	Targeted Time	Date
1		Initiation	Contract Review			
2		Initiation	Open Project in system			
3		Initiation	Request for creating Project Home (folder) and request to assign Project Administrator			
4		Initiation	Request for Performance Bond to Finance (if applicable)			
5		Initiation	Request for Advance Payment Bond to Finance (if applicable)			
6		Initiation	Prepare Project Charter			
7		Initiation	Identify Stakeholders and prepare Stakeholder management plan			
8		Initiation	Obtain Project Resources (Team)-Mobilisation			
9		Initiation	External Kick off Meeting with Client			
10		Initiation	Internal Kick off Meeting with Project Team and Management			
11		Initiation	Scope Verification			
12		Initiation	Set Project KPIs			

PROJECT MANAGEMENT CHECKLIST-STEP BY STEP PROJECT ACTIVITIES

No.	Project Stage	Process Group	Checklist	Status Yes/No/NA	Targeted Time	Date
13		Initiation	Data Collection			
14		Initiation	Issue Notice of Intent			
15		Planning	Prepare RACI Matrix			
16		Planning	Set Project Communication Protocol & Prepare Communication Management Plan			
17		Planning	Prepare Project Management Plan			
18		Planning	Approval of Project Plan (Internal/external)			
19		Planning	Prepare Baseline Schedule			
20		Planning	Prepare Project Budget			
21		Planning	Prepare List of Deliverables			
22		Planning	Prepare Document Control Register			
23		Planning	Identify Initial Project Risks			
24		Planning	Prepare Risk Register			

PROJECT MANAGEMENT CHECKLIST-STEP BY STEP PROJECT ACTIVITIES

No.	Project Stage	Process Group	Checklist	Status Yes/No/NA	Targeted Time	Date
25		Planning	Prepare Inter Discipline document squad check			
26		Planning	Prepare Document Control List			
27		Planning	Prepare Project Documents Checker and approver List			
28		Execution	Monthly Progress Report (External)			
29		Execution	Weekly/Bi weekly Progress Report			
30		Execution	Internal Progress Meeting			
31		Execution	External Progress Meeting			
32		Execution	MOMs (Internal & External meetings)			
33		Execution	Prepare stage wise Design Reports			
34		Execution	Prepare BOQ & Tender Documents			
35		Execution	Prepare Cost Estimate			
36		Monitoring & Control	Project Design Gate Reviews (at each stage)			

PROJECT MANAGEMENT CHECKLIST-STEP BY STEP PROJECT ACTIVITIES

No.	Project Stage	Process Group	Checklist	Status Yes/No/NA	Targeted Time	Date
37		Monitoring & Control	Review Risk list and update Risk Register (Each Stage of the Project)			
38		Execution	Lesson Learned Sessions (Each Stage of Project)			
39		Monitoring & Control	Project Internal Audit after 50% project completion			
40		Monitoring & Control	Update Project Financial Forecast			
41		Monitoring & Control	Prepare Justification or prepare recovery plan If project slips or creep			
42		Monitoring & Control	Monitor Man-Hours & Budget spent			
43		Monitoring & Control	Monitor Project Progress			
44		Monitoring & Control	Evaluate Scope change (if any)			
45		Monitoring & Control	Get approval of scope change from client			
46		Monitoring & Control	Implement only approved changes			
47		Close out	Send CSR (Client Satisfaction Report) to client			
48		Close out	Evaluate CSR with Management			

PROJECT MANAGEMENT CHECKLIST-STEP BY STEP PROJECT ACTIVITIES

No.	Project Stage	Process Group	Checklist	Status Yes/No/NA	Targeted Time	Date
49		Close out	Prepare Close out Report			
50		Close out	Project Post Mortem			
51		Close out	Ensure all invoices have been paid			
52		Close out	Complete job completion form			
53		Close out	Request the project closure			
54		Close out	Project Archiving			
55		Finance	Generate Invoices			
56		Finance	Follow-up with Finance and Client			
57	❖ Milestone	Execution	Submission of Design Reports to Client			
58	❖ Milestone	Execution	Submission of BOQ & Cost Estimate to Client			
59	❖ Mile Stone	Execution	Submission of Tender Documents to Client			
60	❖ Mile Stone	Execution	Documents submission to Authorities for obtaining NOCs			
61	❖ Mile Stone	Execution	Obtain Approvals from Authorities			
62	❖ Mile Stone	Execution	Obtain Approvals from Client			

PROJECT MANAGEMENT CHECKLIST-STEP BY STEP PROJECT ACTIVITIES

No.	Project Stage	Process Group	Checklist	Status Yes/No/NA	Targeted Time	Date
63						
64						
65						
66						
67						
68						
69						
70						
71						
72						
73						
74						
75						
76						

❖ Blank sheet provide for extra activities

www.ingramcontent.com/pod-product-compliance
Lightning Source LLC
Chambersburg PA
CBHW080438220526
45465CB00009B/3338